Thomas Swaim, John Livingston Janeway, Jacob Petit Dailey

Discourses memorial of Abraham Lincoln

Thomas Swaim, John Livingston Janeway, Jacob Petit Dailey

Discourses memorial of Abraham Lincoln

ISBN/EAN: 9783337818968

Printed in Europe, USA, Canada, Australia, Japan

Cover: Foto ©ninafisch / pixelio.de

More available books at **www.hansebooks.com**

DISCOURSES

MEMORIAL

OF

ABRAHAM LINCOLN,

SIXTEENTH PRESIDENT OF THE UNITED STATES,

Delivered in Flemington, N. J.,

BY

THE PASTORS OF THE DIFFERENT CHURCHES,

ON

WEDNESDAY, APRIL 19th, 1865.

———————

PUBLISHED BY THE CITIZENS.

———————

Lambertville, N. J.:
CLARK PIERSON, PRINTER, "BEACON" OFFICE.
1865.

BY

REV. THOMAS SWAIM,

Pastor of the Baptist Church.

DISCOURSE.

"The beauty of Israel is slain upon thy high places. How are the mighty fallen!—II SAMUEL, 1 : 19.

The occasion which calls us together is of the most sadly-solemn and impressive character.— A nation is in mourning!—mourning for their honored and beloved chief, so suddenly, shockingly and mysteriously removed by death. Let all party feelings and other inferior considerations be laid aside as unworthy this sacred hour, that we may do honor to the illustrious dead and to our own citizenship by suitable expressions of sorrow. And let us fervently invoke the divine blessing on this day, both here and throughout the land, that this heavy affliction may be sanctified to all the nation. The foul deed which laid low in death our good and noble president, has no parallel in history. For enormity of conception and villainous execution it stands alone in horror, when viewed as to the station and character of the high mark. That one so good, so upright, so magnanimous, and so untiring in his devotion to the nation's interests, regardless of sections or classes, should be made the victim of such a fiendish conspiracy, was a stunning blow to all loyal hearts throughcut the land. In the strong language of a public journal, of well-known hostility to the administration from the first, may be justly inferred the horror of this shock upon all minds. "It is as if a pall overhung the land, and in the shadow of it dwelled a chilled and awe-struck people. A brotherhood of sorrow—sorrow so poignant that it makes strong men weep and veteran soldiers shudder—has brought all classes and all parties to the drear level of companions in misfortune. Our city looks like a vast burial-ground, whose monuments are hung with the symbols of woe, and along whose avenues a million mourners pace silently in the solemn consciousness of bereavement. It is not only the flags flapping at half-mast in the drizzling rain, or the gloomy vistas of craped facades, that leave the impression of universal mourning, for in the sombre looks and thoughtful sadness of our citizens, their downcast eyes, their subdued tones, we find the most impressive tokens of the popular distress.

" And indeed it has rarely happened that a people have been visited with such *cause* for lamentation. Had it pleased God by disease or accident to take from us our chief magistrate, the shock would have been less. But to see him stricken down by the brutal rage of an assassin, murdered at the very threshold of the gate of peace he was about to open, abruptly hurled from his sphere of usefulness at the crisis of the Republic's fate, is such a misfortune, all that is horrible and pitiable and calamitous has been concentrated into one fatal moment to overwhelm the country with affliction. Oh!

the disgrace of it, the shame of it, the peril of it, if ever that crime should be identified with the American character!" *

If this forcible expression from the leading journal of the most persistent opposition to the administration of our late president be a fair index of the feeling of the party represented, then we justly declare that a *whole nation is in mourning.* And the shock will be felt by the good and the true in other lands. The down-trodden victims of despotism in distant realms will heave a heavier sigh when the sad tidings break upon their ears. No event on this continent has ever produced a more profound sensation in Europe than will this hideous tragedy. As the champion of freedom to all classes and conditions of people the world over, President Lincoln has been enthusiastically recognized by the struggling masses of both continents. Truly, we may apply the language of the text : "The beauty of Israel is slain upon thy high places. How are the mighty fallen!" In moral excellence of character he may be likened unto the beauty of Israel—mighty in his acts and influence, and slain upon the high places of a great nation. Without any special regard to method in our discourse, let us briefly trace *the course and character of our late president and glance at the opening prospects of his successor.*

The life of Abraham Lincoln has now passed into imperishable history. He was one of the truest types of our free American institutions.

---

* New York Daily News, April 17th, 1865.

2

With no hereditary nobility or privileged classes, there is here no royal road to greatness as
in other lands. The door to honorable promo-
tion and unlimited success in every walk of
life is left wide open to merit, as well in the
lower as in the higher classes; and the worthy
poor have oftener gained honorable distinction
in our country than the rich. As wealth, and
ease, and luxury, enervate natural vigor and
take away stimulus to exertion, so poverty, when
associated with virtue and talent, impels to lofty
endeavor, and necessity often becomes the joyful
mother of successful invention. Of very humble parentage and of the most limited advantages of education or society, Abraham Lincoln
rose merely by the force of his peculiar genius
and sterling merit—rose from a poor boy, step
by step, from one position of trust and honor to
another, until he reached the highest in the gift
of the greatest nation on earth. When but a
lad, managing the little farm of his infirm father
with discretion, afterwards taking charge of a
mercantile business, and trading ventures down
"the great river" to New Orleans, studying law
and teaching school, filling different county and
state offices with increasing popularity, afterwards sent to the general congress—in all these
positions he acquitted himself with honor be-
longing to each.

Thus was he being gradually fitted by trials,
and toils, and knowledge of all classes of society
in both sections of our country, slave and free,
and experience in different kinds of business, for
a position the most difficult and hazardous, in

the most critical period of a mighty struggle. Wonderfully was he fitted for this position, for which no one could be adapted without some such training and the attainment of a like character. Formed as to natural parts and led through a thorough discipline by Divine Providence, he was obviously raised up of God and brought to the government for such a time as this. The approaching crisis of this great nation, in the muttering threats of disunion and civil strife on his election, he appreciated as well, perhaps, as any one living. And when summoned by the voice of the people, which he interpreted as the voice of God as well, to the high post of duty, he was not the man to hesitate or falter on account of threats or danger, nor could he go forward without the deepest solicitude. He measured well the mighty portents of the times. As the ship in heavy seas feels the tremendous strain in every timber and is straitened in all her cordage, so did the President elect realize in anticipation the possible perils of his position, when leaving his peaceful home in the west for the great metropolis, to assume the chief magistracy. In that parting address to his loved neighbors he reminded them that as the "Father of his country," the immortal Washington, did not succeed in the Revolutionary struggle without leaning upon Divine Providence, so did he not expect success without like help; "therefore, my friends," said he, *"pray for me."* If ever prayers were needed for a country, they were then; and if ever prayers for rulers were answered, they have been for him.

It was a dark day in our history, although we have seen many a dark one since. No man ever took the inaugural oath with a more sincere desire or determined purpose to fulfill it with fidelity to all concerned. He knew no section or party in such a way as to interfere. He aimed to pacify the excited, and harmonize all by promising that each and all should have fair play under his administration. After exhausting all the powers of impartial statesmanship, he calmly met the issue. When war was thrust upon him by armed traitors, and *not till then*, did he resort to force. Not until our glorious flag was shamefully fired upon, our common property stolen, our treasury robbed, the public forts, arsenals, munitions, vessels, and everything the dastardly traitors could lay their hands upon, were seized as only thieves and assassins take; not till our brave officers and soldiers were shot at with deadly purpose; not till outrages the most provoking and insults the most unendurable were heaped upon us by perjured villains, did the new president resort to coercion. Then did he only aim to retake what was stolen. And what, think you, would our iron-hearted Jackson have been doing all that time. I tell you, my friends, but what you and all men know too well, he would have hung these plotters of treason as high as Haman, as fast as the forms of law would have allowed, *perhaps a little faster*, and all the people would have said, Amen! But our mild and merciful president trusted in God and in the righteousness of his cause. War of defence was begun,

which soon became of necessity a war of offence.
In his own inimitable language: " Both parties deprecated war, but one of them would
make war rather than let the nation survive,
and the other would accept war rather than let
it perish, and the war came."*
Long and hard did our faithful chief try to
save the Union *with slavery*. He honestly tried.
But to his mind it proved of no avail. It seemed as if Heaven had a controversy with our government on account of this accursed institution.
Disasters and defeats attended our arms, and
foreign nations regarded us as alike implicated
in the perpetuation of what they branded our
national sin. With a full view of the whole
case, believing with many others that slavery
was the corner stone and abutment of the rebellion, as it was distinctly avowed by one of its
highest functionaries, and after weighing the
subject well, our God-fearing and upright President decided to alter his policy, and try to save
the Union *without slavery*. He gave all parties
fair notice of his determination, and kindly coun-
seled them beforehand to prepare for this coming change. Anything consistently with justice
and the public welfare which he could do to help
them save their property from pecuniary loss and
their country from desolation, he was ready to do.
Like a patriarch regarding the interests of all
his household or tribe, so did " Father Abraham" look with patriarchal tenderness upon the
wide-spread interests of his great family. History will in her own time award him his high

---

* Inaugural Address, March 4th, 1865.

3

meed of praise for this unparalleled impartiality of his character. But, according to the old classic proverb, " whom the gods mean to destroy they first make mad," the traitors seemed to be given up to madness and blindness. Taking advantage of the very goodness of the president, they whet their anger to a keener edge, and plunged with the greater desperation into the horrors of civil war. Making this the excuse. they appealed to the satellites of slavery everywhere for sympathy and aid. Shame to old England and all her bright memories, that many among her highest in authority lent the full benefit of their aid and sympathy to this slavemongers' rebellion. Shame to her colony on our border, that she harbored our enemies ; and *still deeper shame to our own loyal states*, that many of their people were found to sympathize warmly with the bloody rebels in their deadly aim at our government, and raising a howl of opposition to this inevitable step of our executive, they labored in every way to embarrass the war.

Slow to begin, our firm president was not the man to turn back or be discouraged. Nothing daunted by all this array of opposition and the fears of faint-hearted friends, he in due course of time put into execution the far-famed *Emancipation Proclamation*. Whatever loss or distress may have accrued thereby to the rebel states they can justly attribute to none but themselves, to their own folly and madness, against the earnest and kindest remonstrance of our kindhearted chief. To their posterity this abolition of slavery will be one of the greatest of blessings, affording them like advantages to those so fully enjoyed in the free states; and to this great nation in all her future history, as well as to the unborn millions of other lands, *this grand march of freedom* will prove glorious beyond present conception. This work of ridding the United States of slavery, this Herculean task of disposing of the great vexed question, which has so long perplexed our statesmen and dishonored our national councils, and perverted our sacred pulpits, and broken asunder the most fraternal ties, this mighty work, the solving successfully of the dark and dangerous problem, was the work of Abraham Lincoln. All the merit attaching to the human instrument belongs to him. *The proclamation of Freedom to four millions of slaves stands confessedly identified with the name of Abraham Lincoln.* It will immortalize that name long, long after all his enemies and decriers and their sympathizers have passed into their merited oblivion. The painting of our American artist, Carpenter, so faithfully portraying the first reading of that paper to the cabinet, should be engraved and hung on the walls of every free home in the world.— The results of that great movement have fully justified the large forecast and profound wisdom of our chief magistrate in making it at the time he did. And it is most refreshing to have, even at this late day, the candid testimony of his bitter and persistent opponents. One of the most able and inveterate of these in review of Mr. Lincoln's administration, acknowledges in this mournful juncture, "Had Mr. Lincoln started with his emancipation policy in 1861, his administration would have been wrecked by the moral aid which would have been given the south by the northern conservatives, including a large part of the Republican party. *Had he refused to adopt the emancipation policy much beyond the autumn of* 1862, *the Republican party would have refused public support to the war, and the south would have gained its independence.*— He has given a signal proof of a strong and manly nature in the fact that although he surrounded himself with the most considerable and experienced statesmen of his party, none of them were able to take advantage of his inexperience and gain any conspicuous ascendency over him. All his chief decisions have been his own ; formed indeed after much anxious and brooding consultation, but in the final result the fruit of *his own independent volition.* He has changed or retained particular members of his cabinet, and endorsed or rejected particular dogmas of his party, with the same ultimate reliance on the decisions of his own judgment. It is this feature of his character which was gradually disclosed to the public view, together with the cautious and paternal cast of his disposition, that gave him his strong and increasing hold on the confidence of the masses. The loss of such a president at such a conjucture is an afflicting dispensation which bows a disappointed and stricken nation in sorrow more deep, sincere and universal, than ever before supplicated the compassion of pitying heaven."*

---

* New York World, April 17th, 1865.

Furthermore, with nothing to begin the war with, he raised up an army than which the world has seen no superior. Out of nothing almost he has created a navy which scarcely has an equal in any quarter of the globe. War's deadly weapons of more formidable character science and art have never conceived. And the dread of this mighty people inspires all kingdoms. With a corresponding improvement in all branches of national wealth and power, our prosperity even in a time of gigantic war, and our unlimited resources, astounds the effete monarchies and routine commerce of the old world.

Shall we be told that *Fortune* has smiled on us merely, or that a benignant *Providence* has favored our cause, and that after chastising us during our struggle for our national sins, He has brought us to that condition where He can consistently crown our arms with final and complete success? Are our thanksgivings due first of all to the God of nations, and under Him do we owe much to others associated in authority ; much to our brave officers and soldiers in arms, much to the patriotism at home, ever busy and generous to support our brave boys in the field? Yes, my friends, let it stand on imperishable record, that, as our sanctuaries have often been opened at the call of our chief magistrate for humiliation or for thanksgiving, as events have required during the war, *we have and do still acknowledge first of all, the divine hand in all our public affairs.* Let the millions of boxes of aid to soldiers and millions of bounty money generously paid for enlistment testify that we have in some measure appreciated the sacrifices of our brave soldiers. Let the pensions and future donations to bereaved families and the prayers and sympathies which will flow on while the objects remain, let all this be our testimony that we acknowledge our debt to all. *But under God, and over all other human instruments, justice must be done to the memory of that great and good man, who, in divine providence, was placed over this great nation and who has with most signal wisdom, ability, justice and humanity, administered our public affairs.* Called to take the helm of the ship of state tossed by fearful storms amid rocks and quicksands, has he not held a steady hand? Who could have done better, begirt with such difficulties and dangers? What proof have we that any other mortal could have done so well? Shall we impugn the wisdom of the all-wise Ruler and Arbiter of nations in the selection of such a man for the crisis? In the absence of such proof and in the face of such divine orderings, what must posterity think of the verdict of such self-appointed judges and mole-eyed partisans, who have decried our noble president as incompetent, forsooth! as vulgar! as tyrannical! as weak! In all charity let them hide themselves in their littleness, and "let the memory of the wicked rot." But what terms can measure the malignity of those who rejoice in this most foul and fiendish murder?

Above all such, my friends, stands the ineffaceable record that this great nation has by the ballot box endorsed his administration as no other has ever been before. God has honored

him as no civil ruler has ever been honored before. And on this day is transpiring a scene
the like of which the world has never before
witnessed. Wide-spread throughout all these
states from the Atlantic to the Pacific—yes, let
it be repeated for our children's children, that
throughout all our cities and towns and villages,
habiliments of mourning drape deeply our sanctuaries of every name, all public buildings,
streets and private dwellings. And never were
such sable signs of sorrow more truly emble-
matic of the deep grief that weighs down the
millions of hearts, too deep indeed for utterance.
The solemn tolling of bells, the deep booming
of cannon, the silent processions, everywhere
flags at half mast and heavily draped, tears
coursing many a bronzed cheek as well as of
maiden fair, mournful dirges, and heavy sighs,
all bespeak one of the mightiest and one of the
tenderest of tributes ever recorded in the annals
of time. Rome never paid such honors to her
dead heroes. Greece never lavished such expressions of sorrow and regret over the remains
of her most illustrious men. Embalmed in a
nation's heart will rest for all time the precious
memory of him whom we honor to day.

Oh! my friends, how the people have learned
to love and honor the name of Abraham Lincoln! The honest hearted people can be trusted when not deceived. The sovereign people
will come right when left to the workings of
their own sound sense and fair feelings. And
the poor freed men have found a father whose
legacy of liberty to them no figures can com-

pute. No wonder that we hear of their gathering the clippings of crape from their rich neighbors and after sewing them together drape their humble cabins in the most unaffected sorrow.— Their loss is great indeed. Yes, my friends, and the time will soon come when our enemies themselves will realize that in the murder of Abraham Lincoln they have destroyed their best friend. Of all he must be mourned sooner or later. His virtues will be remembered while his faults will be forgotten. Some faults he had, of course, as he belonged to the race of human and fallible beings. But where are the human hyenas or vampires, who will dig them out of the grave to regale themselves with now?

The place is *holy* ground,
Where Death holds solemn court,
Away, discordant sound!
Away, *unkindly* thought!
That pale and lifeless clay,
Defenceless now doth lie.
Let Pity have her sway!
And heaven-born charity!

Thus brief and imperfect as this memorial of our late beloved and lamented president must be, prepared as it has been on the shortest notice, yet this may suffice to recall his well-known course and character as a public man. In this capacity he is more generally known, and with this our public services are chiefly concerned. Still it must afford no small gratification to all his friends to be assured that in his private character, as the head of a family, as a friend and companion, he stood high in the estimation of all who enjoyed the privilege of

intimate acquaintance. Perfectly upright, in-
genuously *honest*, magnanimous to a fault, and
in all the better qualities of human nature he
had few equals, and *no superiors*. More
than all, my friends, it is interesting to know
that he was a sincere christian. On good
authority it is reported that *he was a man of
prayer*. Like the immortal Washington, he
leaned on the Almighty arm for support, and
cherished a simple faith in the Great Redeemer
to whom he had given his heart. Tenderly
trained up by pious parents, who were Kentucky
Baptists of the good old stock, he ever inclined
to the solid faith of his loved parents. But he
did not become an open and decided christian
until after the battle of Gettysburg. Standing
on that bloody field, his heart was wrung with
anguish at the scene of carnage there spread
out, and the deep exercises of his soul were
sanctified by the Holy Spirit. We fervently
hope that this current report is true, and we
have no reason for disbelieving it. If his private life corresponded with his public course,
we must believe it, for he acknowledged God
in every step he took. He distinctly avowed
his dependence on the divine favor, and God
seems to have recognized and approved of his
course. The christian ministry he treated with
all due respect and gravely considered their
many counsels. In company with a hundred
of our clergy, delegates from the Baptist Anni-
versaries, held in Philadelphia, May, 1864, we
waited upon the President at the White House,
heard him respond briefly and most kindly to

the address presented him, and had the pleasure of a cordial shake of the hand from him. Thus he treated all similar delegations as the servants of the most High God. All honor to his name. His death, viewed from the human side, was a murder of the most aggravated character. There seems to have been a conspiracy, in which many were bound, with designs upon the lives of all the officers of the government. And there were many accessories to the assassination, *before the fact.* But how needless that there should be accessories *after the fact.* Yet in the eye of the divine law all who are pleased or gratified with this murderous deed are accessories after the fact. " O, my soul, come not thou into their secret ; unto their assembly mine honor, be not thou united." " Hide me from the secret council of the wicked, from the insurrection of the workers of iniquity." Viewed as a dispensation of divine providence, which is its most important aspect, this event seems dark and mysterious. Why it was permitted when a nation was looking to him with the utmost confidence, we can learn only as Providence develops.— *Permitted,* it was, for every man is immortal till his work is done, or his appointed course is run. Often before was his life in danger, but his work was not then done. Now that God allowed his life to be taken, it is obvious that his work was done, and *he has done a great work for us.* His part he finished, and finished well. He is safe to history, and will take his place among the most illustrious of the human race.

Most infamously assassinated by a tool of the

rebel chiefs, was it not permitted that the *diaboli-cal spirit* of the rebellion should be displayed in the strongest light, that our hatred of it might be so intensified that we might be prepared to deal with it as it deserves. It was essential in the divine plan, seemingly, that a man of the gentle mould of Abraham Lincoln should be in power during the war, fitted to bear all things with patience, from enemies of every class, in open arms and secret disguise; and that he should at the same time stand with firmness against all discouragements (though the people's heart should often utterly fail them) and all temptations, flattery and threats, that he should feel for the poor and the oppressed, and alike regard the interests of opposite extremes and keep all classes in sufficient harmony to carry the war successfully through. All this he has done, my friends, doubtless as no other man on God's earth could have done. Wonderful man!

But the war being now virtually ended, and another and difficult work of reconstructing the dilapidated temple of justice and liberty to be accomplished, perhaps in the same divine plan it may require a man of less yielding nature and of sterner mould. One man can do but one great thing, and for one man's fame the glory of our illustrious deceased will be enough. Another must enter upon the next grand achievement of reconstruction, and one is called who from personal experience and long observation of the growth of this great rebellion, its cause and course, and forecasted consequences, may be justly fitted to deal with treason according to its deserts as the highest crime, and thus save the country from any future rebellion. Those who live long enough will see if this be so.

But to those who are so deeply conscious of our almost irreparable loss, and who tremble for the jostled ark of the republic, we say listen a moment to some of the last words of that nobleman of nature who succeeds to the presidential chair, uttered after the news came of the fall of Richmond.

" You must indulge me in making one single remark in connection with myself. At the time the traitors in the senate of the United States plotted against the government and entered into a conspiracy more foul, more execrable, and more odious than that of Cataline against the Romans, I happened to be a member of that body, and as to my loyalty stood alone among the senators from the southern states. . I was then and there called upon to know what I would do with such traitors, and I want to repeat my reply here. I said if we had an Andrew Jackson he would hang them as high as Haman. But as he is no more, and sleeps in his grave in his own beloved state, where traitors and treason have even insulted his tomb and the very earth that covers his remains, humble as I am, when you ask me what I would do, my reply is, I would arrest them, I would try them, I would convict them, and I would hang them. All that I have, life, limb and property, have been put at the disposal of the country in this great struggle. I have been in camp, I have been in the field, I have been everywhere where this great rebellion was; I have pursued it until I believe I can now see its termination. Since the world began there never has been a rebellion of such gigantic proportions, so infamous in character, so diabolical in motive, so entirely disregardful of the laws of civilized war. It has introduced the most savage mode of warfare ever practiced upon the earth. One word more and I have done. I am in favor of leniency, but in my opinion evil doers should be punished. Treason is the highest crime known in the catalogue of crimes; and for him that is guilty of it, I would say death is too easy a punishment. My notion is that treason must be made *odious*, that traitors must be punished and impoverished, their social power broken, though they must be made to feel the penalty of their crimes. Hence, I say this: the halter to influential, intelligent traitors; but to the honest boy, to the deluded man, who has been deceived into the rebel ranks I would extend leniency. Death to the conspirators, clemency to their victims. I hold, too, that wealthy traitors should be made to remunerate those men who have suffered as a consequence of their crimes—Union men who have lost their property, who have been driven from their homes beggars and wanderers among strangers. *We have put down these traitors in arms; let us put them down in law, in public judgment, and in the morals of the world.*"

These plain and noble words have the true ring, and coming from such a man as Andrew Johnson, the Tennessee patriot, with such a glorious record, they fill us with confidence in

our new president. We can trust him to de il
with traitors and their victims.

And now, my friends, in conclusion, as the
God of our fathers has brought us thus far
through the Red Sea of our troubles, almost
dry shod in comparison with our enemies, He
will bring us safe into the promised land, while
this worse than Pharaoh, the arch traitor and
his hosts, will be drowned in the deep waters.
Where now is that arch traitor and his satellites ? A fugitive from justice, a vagabond upon
the earth, with a brand more infamous than
Cain's upon his brow. His fellow conspirators
are either slain in battle, or in exile, or in prison, or peeled and scattered ; all are more than
ruined—branded with eternal infamy—and the
territories of rebels are greatly desolated, while
the loyal states are in comparative prosperity.
Let us thank God and take courage.

Yes, let us still trust in God, who will overrule for greater good this most sad calamity
which we mourn to-day. Let us rally round
our new president and continue to support our
government. Let us honor all the noble dead,
who in prison, camp, hospital, or on the battle
field, or elsewhere, have fallen in our behalf;
and first of all of them our good and noble President, *the second father of his country, the martyr
of Liberty, the restorer of the Republic, now no
more among us, but embalmed in a grateful nation's tears.*

BY

REV. J. L. JANEWAY,

Pastor of the Presbyterian Church.

DISCOURSE.

I form the light and create darkness; I make peace and create evil; I, the Lord, do all these things:—ISAIAH 45: 7.

Only a few years since and this nation was in the enjoyment of unexampled prosperity. Long years of peace had enabled us to develop the wonderous resources of the land. Riches springing from a country great in extent, abounding in great wealth, a rich soil and varied climate; aided by a wide stretchy commerce, carried into every sea and to every land, poured the wealth of land and sea into our lap. Living under a form of government well adapted not only to secure the happiness and welfare of the people, but also to bring forth their energies and strength, we had risen in a few years to a pitch of power and prosperity unexampled in the history of the world. We had achieved a name among the nations second to none, and were universally respected or feared. The skies were bright over us, no cloud appeared to obscure the sun of our national prosperity. The nation seemed as though long years of light and joy were before it, and a still brighter future opened to the view. Statesmen and political economists both united in presenting glowing pictures of our future greatness, which should far outstrip the past.

7

But lo ! dark clouds began to appear, the low muttering notes of the coming storm broke bodingly on the ear. Ambitious men, spoiled by prosperity, were heard breathing dissatisfaction and discontent. Secession erected its foul form and raised its destructive hand to tear down the pillars on which our national fabric rested.— State after state listened, and instead of seeking redress in the Union and according to the constitution, in an evil hour attempted to dissolve the national existence, seizing the national armories, and banding together, they stood arrayed in arms against the government. A dread and fearful calm, portentous of the coming storm, ensued, while the dark clouds gathered a thicker blackness. The storm broke suddenly, the traitor blow was struck, the national flag was hauled down from the beleaguered fortress by the little band, compelled to yield through famine and vastly overnumbering foes. The nation awoke to find itself assaulted, its life endangered, its capitol at the mercy of its enemies, and the demon of war spreading its black wings to sweep over the land. Dark days of gloom and civil strife with its varying issues ensued. A struggle of the most tremendous magnitude came upon us. During four long years the nation poured forth its treasures, and rivers of blood flowed.

All are familiar with its history, its dark days of reverse and its bright days of victory. But who can tell the bitter agony of the watching ones at home anxiously waiting in fear and trembling lest the dread news of loved ones fallen should be brought to their ears. Who can tell the agony of the dying ones on the battle field, the pain and languishing of the sick and wounded in hospital, who can gather up and group in one great whole the maimed of these years of war. Who can write out or utter the anxiety of the nation, toiling, suffering, yet patiently enduring all, determined, come what may, to maintain its national existence and unity.

But after four years of fearful struggle, bright streaks of light stream up amid the darkness, the clouds are rifted asunder, not here and there but all through the sky, victory follows victory all over the field, till at length the last stronghold yields, the capital of the foe is taken, the army closely pursued is compelled to surrender and the dark clouds are rent asunder. Tokens of coming peace are most gladly seen and hailed. The national heart rejoices, a frenzy of delight spreads over the land, illuminations and other evidences of the great joy are everywhere seen, while all through the land the people are preparing for a still greater demonstration of their joy.

But suddenly a dark thick cloud comes over the scene, the electric wires flash over the land the dread intelligence that he who had for four terrible years guided the nation, and to whom it was looking and trusting to lead it forth by wise and conciliating counsels to an established peace, is no more; struck down in a moment by the fell blow of the dastardly assassin. The nation so lately exultant mourns its loss. Universal lamentation is on all the land ; the marks of national woe meet us at every step. And we are met this day to mingle our sorrows with our fellow citizens, because they bear to the tomb the lifeless remains of the late chief magistrate. It is a day of darkness and gloom, and sorrow broods on the great heart of the nation. And there is good ground for it; twice before the chief magistrate of the nation has been smitten down by death with his robes of office on, and the nation sorrowed, but not as it sorrows to-day. It felt the blow, but not as it feels it to-day. Then it came as the ordinary visitation meets men by disease; now it is the hand of the fell assassin striking him down in his full health and strength. It was a cold blooded murder, deliberately planned and carried out. Nothing relieves the terrible blackness of the crime.— Never before in our history has such an event transpired, and but seldom in the world's history. The manner of the President's death appealed to the American heart; we cannot but be saddened, we cannot but be oppressed, we cannot but sympathize with each other over the nation's loss.

And then, too, the time adds to the intensity of the blow. After four long years of bloody strife, with its varying issues, its defeats and victories, just as victory after victory had seemed to assure us of coming peace, and when we all hoped that the conciliating and kind policy of the President would tend to win back to their allegiance our foes in a moment, at the very commencement of the course adopted, he from whom we hoped such things is laid low in death. We feel it to be a great national calamity, and how can we help being sad.

Besides this, he had been tried for four years. The country knew him and had proved him. They knew his character ; that no man in the administration was so familiar with all the details of the war, with all its varied features, and that, therefore, he of all in power, seemed best adapted to manage it. But now a new man and untried (at least in the present sphere) must take up the work. And what questions come crowding upon the oppressed national heart? Will he be equal to the emergency? Will he be able to master and comprehend its details? Will he be able so readily to enter on the work, and grasp it as thoroughly? And a sad weight comes over us and oppresses us. We all wish he could have been spared, but it cannot be.— His voice is hushed in death ; his heart, which throbbed for the nation, has ceased to throb, and his watchful eye that scanned the political horizon, watching for the nation's well-being, is closed forever. He has passed away from earthly labors ; he can avail us nothing in the future. His memory, his example, his past labors, alone remain.

But there was that in the man which commended him to the nation, that endeared him to the people. His mind, clear and vigorous, strong and practical, enabled him to come to a clear apprehension of the subject before him and to state it clearly and simply to the public mind.

Honest and sincere in his conduct as a statesman, he desired to know and do right. He

might be mistaken, for he was but a man, but his
conclusions if wrong were the errors of the
head, not of the heart. He desired sincerely
the welfare of his country, and pursued it according to the light he had, earnestly, faithfully,
steadfastly, according to his deliberate judgment. He could not be hurried faster than he
thought he saw the way clear and plain before
him. Placed in a position such as none before
him had occupied, surrounded by all the usual
responsibilities of the chief magistrate, and to
these superadded a thousand fold greater ones
caused by the rebellion, entering upon his offi-
cial duties, at the very moment that the country was crumbling to pieces at his feet, he
grasped steadfastly and unfalteringly the reins
of government. In his inaugural, endeavoring
by mild and conciliating words and declarations
to arrest the rebellion and win back the disaf-
fected ; but firmly enunciating the fact, that
the national flag and authority must be restored
to all the fortresses and over all the states (I am
stating facts,brethren, I allude not to the causes),
slowly but surely the pledge was redeemed, for
he died not, till the winds had caught up and
spread out the folds of the flag on Sumpter, and
the cradle of secession and the capital of the so-.
called confederacy had both surrendered. And
when he died, all the states, save one, were
forced to feel the authority of government, and
the path to peace was opening wide and free.
  Plain and unostentatious, free from pride, he
was of easy access and ready to meet his fellow
citizens kindly and familiarly. Raised to the

highest office in the gift of the people, he was not elated, but was as simple and free as the lawyer of Springfield. There might seem ostentation to the stranger at first sight, as he saw him accompanied by his body-guard, a sight never before seen here, but this was the suggestion of others, not his own, and his death has proved how well grounded their fears for his personal safety were. Only last evening I met in one of the journals an incident illustrative of this trait. In conversation with an artist, at that time employed on some national work, the conversation being a familiar one, had turned on authors and their works. The President remarked that years before he had met a piece of fugitive poetry, the author of which he had long desired to know, but had been unable to find out. The piece had pleased him so much that he had committed it to memory. Then, half closing his eyes, he repeated the following beautiful lines :

OH! WHY SHOULD THE SPIRIT OF MORTAL BE PROUD?

Oh, why should the spirit of mortal be proud?
Like a swift, fleeting meteor, a fast-flying cloud,
A flash of the lightning, a break of the wave,
He passeth from life to his rest in the grave.

The leaves of the oak and the willow shall fade,
Be scattered around and together be laid;
And the young and the old, and the low and the high
Shall moulder to dust and together shall lie.

The infant a mother attended and loved ;
The mother that infant's affection who proved ;
The husband that mother and infant who blessed,
Each, all, are away to their dwellings of rest.

The hand of the king that the sceptre hath borne ;
The brow of the priest that the mitre hath worn ;

The eye of the sage and the heart of the brave,
Are hidden and lost in the depths of the grave.

The peasant, whose lot was to sow and to reap ;
The herdsman, who climbed with his goats up the steep ;
The beggar, who wandered in search of his bread,
Have faded away like the grass that we tread.

So the multitude goes, like the flower or the weed
That withers away to let others succeed ;
So the multitude comes, even those we behold,
To repeat every tale that has often been told.

For we are the same our fathers have been ;
We see the same sights our fathers have seen—
We drink the same stream and view the same sun—
And run the same course our fathers have run.

The thoughts we are thinking our fathers would think ;
From the death we are shrinking our fathers would shrink ;
To the life we are clinging they also would cling :
But it speeds for us all, like a bird on the wing.

They loved, but the story we cannot unfold ;
They scorned, but the heart of the haughty is cold ;
They grieved, but no wail from their slumber will come ;
They joyed, but the tongue of their gladness is dumb.

They died, aye ! they died ; we things that are now,
That walk on the turf that lies over their brow,
And make in their dwellings a transient abode,
Meet the things that they met on their pilgrimage road.

Yea ! hope and despondency, pleasure and pain,
We mingle together in sunshine and rain ;
And the smile and the tear, the song and the dirge,
Still follow each other, like surge upon surge.

'Tis the wink of an eye, 'tis the draught of a breath !
From the blossom of health to the paleness of death ;
From the gilded saloon to the bier and the shroud—
Oh why should the spirit of mortal be proud ?

His manner showed that it had touched a corresponding chord in his own heart.
He was eminently kind and forgiving in his

disposition ; he was free from malice. Maligned, traduced, called by the most opprobrious epithets by the south ; insults of the most stinging character heaped upon him, well calculated to make a deep impression, yet they seemed to fall off from him as harmlessly as shot from an iron clad. He felt kindly to them in spite of all, and would have gladly received and pardoned them. No one can look at his conduct and fail to see this trait standing out in bold relief.

But above all, he was a christian man. He recognized God, as no one before him, for long years, had done ; never since the days of the Father of his country ; as his last inaugural, which some, in bad taste and less piety, have derided, because of this dependence on and distinct recognition of his superintending Providence over nations and his control of their destinies, clearly proves. He looked to the Redeemer as a sinner and professed to have found mercy through his merits. That he was sincere, we believe ; and we trust he has laid aside the labors, the toils and anxieties of life, for an eternal rest in heaven.

He has passed away ; we shall see him no more, til! the risen dead appear before the great Judge. We mourn his loss. The voice of party is hushed, and the national heart throbs in anguish at his tomb. Darkness and gloom sit alike upon city, town and hamlet, for the standard bearer has fallen.

What means this? Whence this terrible evil that has come, dashing from our hands the cup of joy and replacing it with sorrow? Are we the sport of some evil being who delights in human woe and who has led us these four years long through war and gloom, and when our heavens were gathering brightness has brought over them another terrible cloud of blackness? And what and when shall the end be?

The text meets and answers these. It tells us that there is but one God. He forms the light and creates darkness ; he makes peace and creates evil ; the Lord doeth all these things.— The good he himself actively brings to pass ; the evil he permits ; he allows it to be done ; but for wise and holy purposes ; while he will so control and overrule it as shall in the end promote and secure a higher good to those who mark his hand and seek his aid. He works in the dark mysteriously, but none the less wisely and kindly. "Clouds and darkness are round about him, but righteousness and judgment are the habitation of his throne." But why? What is the reason of the blow? I feel incompetent, brethren, to interpret God's providences. I prefer humbly to watch and wait the end, when God himself shall make plain what is now so dark and mysterious. But still, I think there are some things which it may be God's design to teach us and which we may safely and not presumptuously infer : and, first, it teaches us not to depend on the instrument. God is the efficient worker—man but the instrument by which he works ; and God is very jealous for his own honor and glory. He forbids us to put our confidence in an arm of flesh ; and may it not be that we have sinned here? May there not have been, nay, was there not, too much reliance on the chief magistrate. How many looked on him as necessary to this crisis, and as though the very salvation of the land depended on him. While there was undoubtedly a reliance on God and a public acknowledgment, was there not underlying it the feeling that our salvation must come through the man, and thus we really distrusted God and gave a part of his glory to the instrument, and now is he not showing us by the removal that he is tied to no instrument, and that he can put aside one and use another? If he wills to accomplish our deliverance, he can and will do it in the way it seemeth good in his sight, and will select such instruments as shall show most clearly that it is of God. Thus he rebukes all false trust and confidence.

Next, we may safely infer that all these things have come upon us because of our sins as a people. Time does not admit more than an allusion to this. We can only say our sins are many and great as a nation, and God will humble us first that he may exalt us afterwards.— He calls us to repentance ; let us heed his voice and turn to him that we may live as a people.

Again, may there not have been in our rejoicings too much forgetfulness of the fearful cost paid for our victories—the blood which has flowed and the anguish and suffering in the field and at home. Oh, let us never forget, whilst we may and should rejoice, the fearful price laid down.

Another lesson taught is, a solemn recognition of God's hand in the event. " Be still and

know that I am God." He has done it. "Shall
there be evil in the city and the Lord hath not
done it!" Not actively, but passively he has
permitted it; not that he approves it. No, he
detests the crime, and even now frowns on
the fell assassin, and though he should escape
the judgment of man, we may feel sure he will
not escape God's righteous judgment.

But let us banish vengeful feelings ; let us
leave to the law the punishment of evil doers ;
aiding and upholding to the extent of our influence and power him, who is God's appointed
minister to execute vengeance, that he bear not
the sword in vain. But mob law and violence
are evils fraught with danger to our free institutions and tend to anarchy and confusion.—
Let us beware how we ever take the law in our
own hands. We are not God's ministers unless
lawfully appointed, and he delegates to us no
authority to punish even the evil doer. In so
doing, we ourselves do wrong. Let the law and
its penalties be duly inflicted upon those who
do evil by those who are appointed to do so.

Another lesson taught us is to sustain the
present chief magistrate. By *God's own act* he
is invested with the robes of office. Uphold his
hand, cheer his heart, give him your earnest
prayers; pray that God may guide, enlighten
and bless him. Many are all wrong here.—
They differ in policy and views from the administration that may be in power (I speak now of
the general principle), but is he any the less the
ruler ; is our country any the less dearer ; is its
good any the less in God's hand? It has always

seemed to me, the opposition party, if they sincerely believe the policy injurious, ought to pray the more earnestly. And how can any man who prays at all, answer it to his God, if he neglects to pray for rulers, when He has commanded us to pray for them. " I exhort, therefore, that first of all, supplications, prayers, intercessions and giving of thanks, be made for all men ; for kings and for all that are in authority ; that we may lead a quiet and peaceable life in all godliness and honesty, for this is good and acceptable in the sight of God our Saviour."

Lastly, let me urge you one and all to repress and keep down that fell demon of evil to our institutions, party spirit. That all men should think alike is too much to expect. That there will be differences of opinion in reference to matters of policy we may expect. Nor is this an evil, nor is this party spirit. But a determination to oppose all measures proposed, to see no good in them and misrepresent them because they originate with the other party, is surely an evil, especially attended, as they are, with a misrepresentation of the motives leading to the policy ;—this fierce denunciation of men and motives because we differ in politics, accusing those whom we meet and trust and respect in the ordinary affairs of life, of the most base and unworthy conduct in politics, because they do not and cannot see as we do. The voice of party is now hushed and men of all parties unite in paying honor to and lamenting the dead.— Is not God rebuking this fell spirit of evil. Oh when shall it cease ! oh when shall our differences in matters of policy, instead of alienating us, only make us more zealous to do our country and each other good!

And now may God bless and sanctify to us as a people these visitations of his hand. Amen.

BY

REV. J. P. DAILEY

Pastor of the Methodist Episcopal Church.

DISCOURSE.

No words are required to explain the object of this meeting to-day. The signs of mourning here and over all the land express the sense of deep sorrow that lies heavy on the nation's heart. Nor can the use of emphatic words and impressive figures deepen the impression of the sad calamity with which the nation is stricken. Yet it may be reasonably expected that the pastor of this church, as a minister of the gospel and as an American citizen, should be willing to say something to his fellow citizens for his country and for his God. We are quite willing to make some very plain remarks, leaving the eulogy and the poetry befitting the occasion to minds more gifted and to tongues more eloquent.

Abraham Lincoln, sixteenth President of the United States, was born July 12th, 1809, and died April 15th, 1865. Physically, he was a man capable of very great endurance, as his almost uninterrupted good health during four years of immense labor, under the pressure of prodigious responsibilities, fully proves. His most striking mental characteristic was great *common sense.* That was the sheet anchor of his practical character. He always seemed to know when to speak and when to act, as well

11

as when not to speak and not to act. Those who listened for words of mere sentiment or looked for actions of mere show from Abraham Lincoln, were simply disappointed. No ruler in any age of the world ever had such great difficulties to solve and to manage as had President Lincoln. But his common sense always seemed to be equal to the occasion. The counterpart of this characteristic was the power of judging correctly. Clear in its profundity and eminent in degree was the judgment of that great man. Prudence was another characteristic, and like the others named, was strikingly permanent and practical. Blunders or mistakes *in action* were very rare with Mr. Lincoln. Any of these that may have appeared in his public life, of the forms of omissions or tardiness, were doubtless caused by the crude and ponderous, but powerful, influences of the age, bearing on a character more thoughtful than impulsive. The controling elements of his *moral* character were *honesty, kindness, patience and patriotism.* All these are important elements in the character of every good citizen, and essential elements in the character of a christian.

As a politician he exhibited great coolness and honesty of purpose, in a policy of great simplicity. In the memorable contest with Mr. Douglas for the senatorship of Illinois, it was shown that those two great men were nearly equal in the confidence of the people of that state. Mr. Douglas carried a majority of the counties and secured the senatorship. Mr. Lincoln had a small majority of the popular vote. Again, in

1860, those same men were before the people of
Illinois as rival candidates for the presidency.
The result then showed the more enduring influence of Mr. Lincoln. He carried the state by a
majority of 11,946 over Mr. Douglas and 4,629
over all opposition. It required a *strong spirit*,
a *clear eye* and a *steady hand* to break a lance
with Mr. Douglas ; and he who could fairly win
in such a contest, need fear no other champion
in the political arena.

The statesmanship of Mr. Lincoln was
brought out under the most trying circumstan-
ces, yet he always seemed to measure the difficulties of his situation with a careful and steady
hand. As President of the United States, he
was the most democratic of all our Presidents.
His policy was the most simple and clear, ever
developed in any administration. No one of
the illustrious line of noble men who have filled
the presidential chair, ever cared so much for
the humbler classes of the people, or opened his
heart or explained his policy so much to the
people, as did President Lincoln. No one of
them ever had half the difficulties to contend
with in his administration. The great questions
of *Slavery*, of *State rights*, and of *Secession*, which
other Presidents had managed to evade or to
compromise, *had to be met* by President Lincoln.

Before he was sworn in as President of the
Union, seven States had sworn themselves out
of the Union, and their traitorous statesmen,
after failing to secure the consent of President
Buchanan to their nefarious scheme, were now
testing their powers of peerless chivalry and of

superlative statesmanship, in a grand double effort on the one hand to befog northern politicians and the new President into an acknowledgment of their maudlin doctrine of State rights, and on the other hand, to starve Major Anderson and his ninety men *into* submission or *out of* Sumpter. Yet Mr. Lincoln, noble and generous man that he was, rejoiced that as yet, there was "nobody hurt," and in his inaugural address told the whole people, and those traitors, too, that there could be no war unless they began it. But the day of compromises had gone by ; and within one month and ten days, to fire the Southern heart, they fired on Sumpter, and fired the whole American heart. Then the war cloud shot forth its lightnings, and its thunders rolled over the world. The President had to grasp the helm and guide the Ship of State through the fiery tempest of four terrible years. Whenever you shall have read a true history of these years of war, you will have a history of the statesmanship of President Lincoln. I pass no eulogy nor make comment on it now ; the time for that is not now. But we may notice some two or three great facts involved in that history, which must be studied now.

1. Four years ago, many of the greatest statesmen in Europe and many equally great in our country, pronounced the attempt to put down the rebellion by force of arms, "a piece of madness." Who is so mad as to hold that opinion now?

2. Then slavery was the giant difficulty, that some *loved, some hated,* but *all feared.* Who fears it now?

3. After being subjected to four years of severest trial, Mr. Lincoln was elected for a second term of four years service at the helm of state. Who regrets that now?

These are some of our opinions of Abraham Lincoln, as *an honest man, a great statesman, and a good president.* But we will give the opinion of others. A body of citizens met a few evenings since and passed the following resolution:

Resolved, That believing Abraham Lincoln as a ruler to have been governed by patriotic motives, honesty of purpose, and an elevated appreciation of the grave and responsible duties imposed upon him in the greatest crisis of our country's history, commanding in so great a degree the confidence of the loyal people of the nation, and exhibiting in the recent events which had culminated in the downfall of the rebellion, a wise, forbearing and magnanimous statesmanship, the exercise of which gave such promise of a speedy and perfect restoration of the National Union, and the spirit and on the principles upon which it was founded, we cannot but regard his sad and untimely decease as a great misfortune to the nation at this critical period.

Now where and by whom do you suppose this resolution was passed? It was passed by a committee of intelligent and powerful politicians who, less than one year ago, in strong and stirring language, intended for the whole American people, denounced Mr. Lincoln as one of the worst of tyrants and his administration as a piece of the worst kind of despotism. It was passed in Tammany Hall, by the general committee, with not one dissenting voice. Who will now doubt the honesty of President Lincoln or pronounce his administration a failure?

But the great and good President Lincoln is dead. He died from being shot in the head, while sitting with his wife and a friend or two, in a theatre in the city of Washington, last Friday night. I am sorry he went to that theatre. After being wounded, he lingered insensible until twenty-two minutes past seven o'clock on Saturday morning, when he died. His death was by a cowardly and diabolical assassination. The act of shooting down that quiet, unsuspecting man, in the presence of his wife, was one of cold blooded and murderous brutality. The author of this horrid crime is one of the vilest of reprobate men ; one of the most miserable beings out of hell. The name or fate of this criminal is not of the greatest importance; still, I would have him arrested, tried, and when proven guilty, made to suffer death. Yet, even for him, would I deprecate all mob violence ; I would not have him suffer one minute of unnecessary torture, as he was, doubtless, the tool of an infernal plot. Let him be put out of the way and let him go to his own place ; let foul vapors and darkness envelop his grave, and let the ghosts of silence be the only sentinels of his memory. But when we come to speak of the responsibility of this crime, we touch the most delicate and fearful part of the whole matter. That he who fired the pistol is directly responsible, no one may doubt. But the question of indirect responsibility, though it may be a delicate one to speak of, is nevertheless one of awful magnitude. God alone may be able to fix the shades and degrees of this responsibility, notwithstanding we cannot, at our peril we cannot, ignore the subject. *It must be studied now*. The habit of speaking evil of political opponents, and es-

.pecially of those in authority, though wide spread and of long standing, is the poison source of many of the bitter streams that reach all classes and all parties of our people, spreading blasting and mildew over all our social, political and moral interests.

Many of us remember the time when Andrew Jackson and Henry Clay were rival candidates for the presidency; how each was represented by his opponents as a deadly enemy to *liberty, morality* and *religion.* Many of the people believed those representations, and were induced to hate the name of Jackson, or of Clay, as long as they lived. Yet we have lived to hear the same Jackson politicians tell us that Henry Clay was a grand old patriot, and the same Clay politicians wish they only had another Jackson.— This folly might be passed with a smile did we not know there is sin against God in it, and did we not see the same deadly spirit still at work, which after eulogizing Jackson and Clay, proceeds to traduce other men as good as they were, just as heartily and just as bitterly as they were traduced. This loose spirit would naturally prevail most where there was the least amount of general intelligence, and where there were other vices and sins to harmonize with it. A man who could feel that it was no sin to deprive a race of men of their liberty and to keep them in perpetual bondage, (without any fault of their own,) would not be likely to see much wrong in depriving other men of their good name and subjecting them to perpetual odium. Thus the thing has grown up to ripeness for

treason and a willingness to shed blood to grati-
fy the feelings it had engendered.

The murder of President Lincoln was part of
a plot to murder others at the same time, and
that plot was but counterpart to another plot, in
the conspiracy to *burn*, *rob* and *murder* in our
northern cities and our northern frontier. Beale
and Kennedy were in concord of spirit with the
assassins of the President and of Mr. Seward.—
And this latter plot was but part of the pro-
gramme in the satanic enterprise of treason, for
the success of the rebellion and the death of the
Union. The war appeared to be nearly ended.
Terms of surrender strangely magnanimous and
liberal to a fault had been accorded to the main
army of rebels. Joy was over all the land.—
But the culminating crime of treason has turned a nation's joy to grief. We are in the house
of God to ask his blessing, while we reflect upon
the lesson to be taken from this solemn event.
Seeing in this *result* of treason the awful *nature*
of that crime, " Let every soul be subject unto
the higher powers, for there is no power but of
God ; the powers that be are ordained of God.
Whosoever, therefore, resisteth the power, resisteth the ordinance of God; and they that resist
shall receive to themselves damnation. For rulers are not a terror to good works but to the
evil." Let us stand rebuked for our political
follies ; repent of them, and henceforth by God's
help " abstain from all appearance of evil." Let
us remember that " the Lord reigneth," that his
wisdom, power and goodness sustain the nation, and President Lincoln was only his min-

ister to us for good. Let us pray more for our rulers, giving no place to the folly that dares to neglect this duty, for fear of exciting that other folly that dares object to prayer for God's blessing upon our rulers. Let us be more honest in our politics, more charitable, more prayerful.— Let us abandon every line of policy that requires us to assent to, or to compromise, or be partakers of other men's sins, no matter how great in political influence, how deep in worldly interest, or how congenial to pride and ambition those sins may be. In trying to correct the errors of opinion or practice among our fellow citizens, let us do all in the spirit of that charity which " suffereth long and is kind, that envieth not, vaunteth not itself, is not puffed up, doth not behave itself unseemly, seeketh not her own, is not easily provoked, thinketh no evil, rejoiceth not in iniquity, but rejoiceth in the truth." As we are all heirs of a good government from our " Father in Heaven," let us be alike faithful to that government. Every true American is both a Republican and a Democrat. A Republican who is not a Democrat, or a Democrat who is not a Republican, is only in part a true citizen. It takes at least two such men to make a full toned American citizen. Republicanism describes the principles of our government. Democracy describes the application of those principles. There is no radical opposition of principle between them; there should be none in practice. They should be cherished in harmony by all citizens. They will always work in harmony while we remain faithful to God and true to the government which he gave to our fathers and to their children.

Let us thank God that this calamity did not fall on the nation in more perilous times; that President Lincoln's eyes were not darkened by death until he had seen the flag of the Union waving at Richmond; nor until he had been able to proclaim to foreign powers that vessels of the United States navy must no longer be subject to regulations degrading them to a level with rebel pirates.

Let us thank God that the sun which rose on the morning that Lincoln died had not reached the noon, before the nation had another President, duly invested with all his authority, surrounded by the same staff of patriotic intelligence, and backed by a national determination, more deep and firm than ever, to sustain the executive and maintain the Union.

Let us be thankful for institutions that do not die when Presidents die, but live while treason plots and rebellion rages, in spite of assassination itself. Regarding these institutions as given unto us by God, and seeing how in his goodness he continues them to us through such threatening calamities, should we not love them more than ever and be willing to make sacrifice in order to transmit them an unimpaired but improved heritage to our children? Let us try to come to a clear and elevated appreciation of that great truth that ought to be the fundamental principle of all statesmanship, that "righteousness exalteth a nation while sin is a reproach to any people," that no policy, or platform, or set of political principles, can take the place of Bible truth, or work so simply and so surely in the exaltation of a nation.

Finally, my friends, in what words can I more appropriately close these remarks than in the words of him to whom we pay these mournful rites of respect to-day.

" With malice toward none, with charity for all, with firmness in the right, as God gives us to see the right, let us strive on to finish the work we are in, to bind up the nation's wounds, to care for him who shall have borne the battle and for his widow and his orphans, to do all which may achieve and cherish a just and lasting peace among ourselves and with all nations."

CPSIA information can be obtained
at www.ICGtesting.com
Printed in the USA
BVHW031408280819
557039BV00006B/789/P